LIVING WITH SECRETS

The Unmasking of the Hidden Identity

SHAMEKA LECOUNT

LIVING WITH SECRETS

The Unmasking of the Hidden Identity

SHAMEKA LECOUNT

LIVING WITH SECRETS
The Unmasking of the Hidden Identity

Printed in the United States of America

Copyright @ 2018 Shameka LeCount

The copyright laws of the United States of America protect this book.
No part of this publication may be reproduced or stored in a retrieval system for commercial gain or profit.

No part of this publication may be stored electronically or otherwise transmitted in any form or by any means (electronic, photocopy, recording) without written permission of the author.

Scripture quotations are taken from the Holy Bible, New Living Translation, copyright © 1996, 2004, 2007, 2013, 2015 by Tyndale House Foundation.
All rights reserved.

Editing: SynergyEd Consulting
synergyedconsulting.com

Cover Design & Marketing: Greenlight Creations
www.glightcreations.com/ glightcreations@gmail.com

Photography: In God's Image
Photographer Tanisha Walker
www.ingodsimage.net

Library of Congress Cataloging-in-Publication Data
ISBN-13: 978-0-9994470-8-6

SHEROPublishing.com
ericaperrygreen@gmail.com
For copies, publishing or bookings, call or text (919) 522-8195

Printing: Impress Print & Graphics Solutions

LIVING WITH SECRETS ~*The Unmasking of the Hidden Identity*

Table of Contents

DEDICATION		5
ACKNOWLEDGEMENT		6
ABOUT THE AUTHOR		9
FOREWORD		11
INTRODUCTION		12
CHAPTER 1	MISSING PIECES	14
CHAPTERS 2	PLEASE, STOP!	31
CHAPTER 3	SILENT TEARS	42
CHAPTER 4	MY BEST FRIEND	52
CHAPTER 5	I CAN SMILE AGAIN	59
CHAPTER 6	MY BITTERSWEET LOVE STORY	67
CHAPTER 7	NOTHING LEFT	84
CHAPTER 8	WHO AM I?	90
CHAPTER 9	MENDING MY BROKEN HEART	96

Dedication

I dedicate this book to my cousin, Rosemary Blackshear. Before she passed away, Rosemary called to encourage me to finish my book. She told me that she wanted a copy of it! While I didn't finish this book before her passing, my dear cousin will always live within the pages.

My cousin and I had our ups and downs but we never left each other's side. Rosemary, thank you for always praying and encouraging me to become better than my circumstances. I know you are looking down from Heaven smiling because I finally finished the book!

You will never know how much you inspired me. I wish you were still here so that we could share our stories together.

I forever love my Rose.

Acknowledgments

To the most important person in my life, my daughter, Aniyah Morton: You are the reason behind me doing everything that I do. Without you, I don't think I would be here today. You are the reason my heartbeats. Thank you for always believing in your mommy. I thank God for my little prayer warrior. He has placed something special in you. Aniyah, I love you to life and if you never remember anything mommy tells you, remember to never let fear stop you from reaching your full potential. I love you and always keep God first in everything you do.

To my mother, Michelle Wesley Murray: Thank you for bringing me into this world. I know that our relationship has not always been the greatest, but know that I love you with everything in my heart. You are much stronger than I sometimes give you credit for. You survived being a mother of eight children. I just want to take this time to let you know that you are an awesome person inside and out. Please know that no matter what, I have your back. I love you girl!

To the person I owe my life, my grandmother, Mary West: Words cannot begin to show my gratitude for what you have done for me. I don't know where I would be if you hadn't made the decision to raise me. Growing up, I never understood why you were so hard on me but, I now know that it was to help mold me into the person I am today. Thank you for always praying for me and encouraging me. You were my shoulder to cry on, when I felt like giving up. Thank you for simply being you. Grandmother, you will never have to worry about anything because I will make sure that you are taken care of. You hold a special place in my heart. I love you Louise.

To my life-saver, my former pastor, Jacqueline Walton: Who knew one simple post, on social media, would lead me to the person that would save my life. When I tell people that you saved my life, they look perplexed. When I came to you I was broken. I remember going to lunch with you and sharing all of myself with you. Not one time did you judge me and I thank you for that. I still hold onto the words that you shared with me.

When I felt like throwing in the towel, God always gave you a word just for me. Thank you for your prayers, encouragement, and for pushing me to reach my destiny. I thank God for placing me under your leadership. I don't trust a lot of people. Pastor Walton, you are someone I trust and can came to about anything. I look up to you because of the God in you. I have never met such a genuine person, in my life. I love you to the moon and back.

About The Author
Shameka LeCount

Shameka LeCount

Shameka D. LeCount is a Certified Life Coach, Educator, and the Founder of Daughters of Divine Destiny. She was born in Brunswick, GA but was raised in Raleigh, NC. She was educated in both McIntosh County and Wake County Public School System. In 2005, she graduated from Needham B. Broughton High School where she received her high school diploma.

Shameka is the mother to a beautiful and energetic little girl name Aniyah. She always states that Aniyah is the reason that she is here today. Her daughter is the main reason why she does what she does.

Shameka felt the need to birth this book, *Living With Secrets*, to help other women, like herself, elevate past their past. She desires to see women released from the things that have stopped them from reaching their full potential. Shameka understands that is not always easy to let go and overcome those things that have hurt you to your core. In the book, Shameka gives women the tips and tools that she used to find her release. She prays that women will see her book as a tool towards their freedom.

Shameka has a heart for helping young girls and women. Through her youth group and community works, she is motivating people from all walks of life. Shameka is focused on helping women proclaim their lives. She wants women to stand up and tell fear that it is no longer welcomed! Shameka encourages other women to share their stories. She wants them to know that their testimonies could save someone's life.

Life throws us some hard punches but with each hit we are capable to keep pushing through.
We are OVERCOMERS!

~ Coach Shameka

You never know what's behind that smile.
She may be ready to give up or hide from the struggle of life.
I encourage you to share some encouragement because you might just save a life.

– Coach Shameka

Forward

Living With Secrets is a must-have to every women's collection. No matter your story there is a chapter, a sentence, or a line for you between these pages. Even as a close friend to the author I was astonished and motivated by her words.

Author Shameka LeCount has opened Pandora's Box and given us a front row seat. In this world where reality is no longer real, the author has written the truth and nothing but the truth, in this page-turning book. No more entertaining catch phrases and hash tags to tweet. Women, we need a friend, a plan and a light to get out of our puddle of sorrows and pity.

Living With Secrets is about the various hurts, pains, and disappointments we often times experience as women. However, it's also about happiness and joys of life. You will feel each of those emotions as you embark on this journey with the Shameka.

The trip through each chapter will be an insight to her healing. You will experience her milestones and achievements. Settle in and enjoy the ride; not to a far away majestic land around the world, but to a theme park called **LIFE** on a roller coaster called emotions. See how faith, family, and real friends can help launch you into your greatest potential after a past of tremendous pain.

~ Demetria Jackson, CCC-SLP

Introduction

Growing up I didn't have a voice. In my household it was you can be seen but not heard. I found it very hard to express myself because of that. I have always been different and never fit in, with the people I tried to befriend. I knew, at a young age, that I had to go through some things so that I could effectively encourage other women, of various ages and walks of life. God had a plan for my life that still shocks me to this day.

Living With Secrets- The Unmasking of the Hidden Identity takes you on a journey of the things that, I have been scared to share for years. Within the pages of this book I only share the things I've been through to help someone else overcome their own life issues.

Finishing this book was tough. It was extremely hard to revisit some of the experiences of my past, but God kept pushing me. Every time I wanted to give up, God sent someone to push me forward and encourage me to, "Get the book done!" I am glad that God gave me the voice to encourage someone else that is on the verge of giving up. I am here to empower and encourage you to release the pain, fear or whatever it is that is keeping you from reaching your destiny.

In this process I had to reveal things I never spoke about to people that were very close to me. I had individuals who were angered, because I finally released the pain that I was holding in for way too many years. I spent plenty of nights crying and pondering whether or not to release my book. After much prayer and coaching, I choose to release my story and my truth.

I can no longer be held hostage to the opinions of others. If anyone is offended or bothered by what is shared, I can offer you my prayers, but can not remain imprisoned to my past. This is the boldness that God has allowed me to now walk in. While I am not here to hurt anyone, my story is... my story. No parts of my account are fabricated. I vow to share the whole truth and nothing but the truth within the pages of this book.

Fasten your seat belts and get ready to go on this bumpy journey with me. I must warn you that as you read my story, you may shed a few tears, but that is okay. Your tears should be those of joy, as I am free from bondage!

Hold on, for we are in this together. I now understand that I am simply one woman representing many. I pray that with every page you read and as you reflect on my healing and transformation, that you too will be blessed with the same and free from bondage.

Remember this, *"We have to stop dwelling on things we can't change. We are moving forward and overcoming life issues one step, one moment, one day, one week and one month at a time. Greater days are ahead of us."* ~ Coach Shameka

Chapter 1: Missing Pieces

As I mentioned previously, I contemplated heavily whether or not I wanted to share my story. I didn't want to be judged or hurt anyone in the process, but at the same time, I could no longer allow others to hinder me from moving forward. I went through too much to not share my testimony with someone else to help them overcome.

The great thing about life is that we can be patient with who we are while we are in the process of becoming who we were predestined to be. For many years I felt like I was so damaged and that I was going to need serious professional help. While there is absolutely nothing wrong with seeking counseling or therapy, I must honestly say that my relationship with God has really sustained me. I know I would not have made it through half of those situations, if it wasn't for the Lord on my side. This is how it all began.

My mother gave birth to me at the young age of twenty. At that time, she already had two other children. Three days after I was born, my mother decided that being a mother of three was too much for her. My mom decided it was best for my paternal grandmother to take care of me. She was a single mother and didn't receive much help from my father. According to my father he was not ready to become a parent and ended up moving out of the state. This left me with missing pieces to my heart. Imagine growing up with neither one of your parents being active in your life. I was even more upset at my mother, for giving me away to my grandmother than at my father moving out of state.

Why, you may ask? The reason being is because every daughter needs her mother to teach her the fundamentals of life and being a woman. I was left to learn all of these things from others or even on my own sometimes. I often tried to make sense of my mother's decision, however, I could never get away from thinking: *Was I not good enough? Was I not pretty enough? Was I a mistake?* Those questions ran through my mind almost daily and I never received a solidified answer to those questions. Now, I realize that she couldn't provide me with the life that I deserved therefore, her only resort was to give me to someone that could.

Another nagging question that I had was, *Why me?* My mother had two other children before me and I often wondered what made her chose me to give away. *Why not them?* This left me to feeling unwanted, abandoned and rejected. The great thing is that as a child, I was always told I was different. I had to deal with the hurt, pain and anger of my mother giving me away. This has enabled me to minister to others who have not forgiven their mother or father for leaving them for whatever reason it may have been.

I remember going visit my mother anytime she wanted me to, but then those visits became few and in between. I was losing my mother right in front of my eyes and there was nothing I could do about it. My mother had an addiction. It led her to prison on several occasions. My father also had an addiction to alcohol and was never really a part of my life. At a young age, I learned that addictions make you forget about the things that truly matter. Addictions come first. They are the only thing that can make the user happy. Addictions caused my mother and father to lose control of their lives.

I knew my mother had a problem and honestly I didn't care. I just wanted her in my life; by my side. As children, when your parents or loved ones are battling sicknesses you really don't understand all they are dealing with. I expected my mother to be around and to love me. I was a child and didn't ask to be here!

I missed being able to share mother/daughter time with my mom. I used to get discouraged when people would discuss the things that they have learned from their parents and I didn't have anything to share. I remember feeling so angry that I didn't get to share the experiences of having a mother. All I ever wanted was to go shopping together, go get our nails done together, have girl talk, and a shoulder to cry/lean on. Now don't get me wrong, we had great times together, but I wanted more from her.

I can remember this one particular time, mother and I went to the beach together. This moment was so special to me because we had no cares of the world. My mother and I walked the beach hand-in-hand, just living in the moment. The only sad part was the fact that we both knew that this was temporary and that we may not get a chance to do this again anytime soon. We sat near the water with our feet on the edge and my mother allowed me to do most of the talking. I shared whatever I wanted. I can remember just crying. I cried not because I was sad, but because I could see that my mother was trying to be all she could be for me, in that moment.

The void of my parents caused severe abandonment issues. Growing up, it was extremely hard for me to trust anyone because I had already lost my trust in my parents. You always think that your parents are going to be the ones to protect you and make sure that nothing ever happens to you. Instead, they were the ones that hurt me the worst.

How can I be a good mother if I never had one? How will I learn who is the right type of males to date if I never had a male figure in my life? Growing up those were the type of questions I used to ask myself repeatedly. I would shut down on people because of the various emotions I felt. I felt abandoned and left to figure life out alone. I was so damaged that I didn't want to be around myself. How could I be so young and yet so damaged? Let me tell you how.

Living with my grandmother I didn't have the luxury of having name brand clothes and shoes or even experiencing a normal childhood. I got what she was able to provide for me and was grateful for it. From time to time, my grandfather would sneak out and get me a pair of name brand shoes. My grandfather's generosity was only when he could afford it. I realized that he and my grandmother were on a fixed income and I was an additional mouth to feed.

My grandmother kept me so sheltered that I felt like I missed out on a lot of my childhood. I wasn't able to hang out with my friends or enjoy a sleepover. If it wasn't involving a family member, I couldn't attend. My grandmother felt that she could keep me safe, if she kept me close to my family and in church. Unfortunately, this is where the majority of my pain came from: church and family.

I don't really think anyone understood how not having my mother in my life affected me in such a major way. My childhood consisted of writing weekly letters to my mother, going to visit my siblings, or from time-to-time, waiting for them to come visit me. I would get so excited to hear from my mother, but I did have times when I was sad about my mother being in prison. I wouldn't wish my childhood on my worst enemy.

I used to hate to tell people where my mother was because I felt like no one understood what I was going through and they just wanted to be nosey. That was a problem for me. I didn't have enough people asking me how I was doing or even telling me they loved me; they only wanted to know where my mother was. No one knew that I was in need of someone to show me attention.

My abandonment hurt didn't stop at home. I was even picked on in school for having absentee parents. When I was teased at school, that's when the thoughts that my mother didn't want me were the loudest. At the age of ten, I could not fully understand why my mother would choose to keep my other two siblings, but not me.

I remember the day my mother told me she was coming home from prison. It was one of the best days of my life. Finally I could kiss and hug her. I just knew she was coming to get me and we would live happily ever after. It was never a day that went by that I didn't think about what it would have been like if I fully had her in my life. I felt like a lot of the things that I went through wouldn't have happened if I was with her.

While I don't remember every experience, there is one particular thing I remember that I would probably never forget. The day before fifth grade graduation my mother was supposed to be released from prison. My mother promised me that she would come to my graduation with bells on her shoes so that I would know that she was there. I was so excited and anxious to see my mother. She never showed up. I searched and searched but couldn't seem to find her. I was heartbroken.

From day one I experienced broken promises from her. So for me, this was my normal. Later on I found out that she wasn't release because of bad behavior. I was definitely hurt. Not only did my mother not get release from prison, but she missed yet another one of the most important days of my life, my graduation.

Why did I have to endure so much pain at a young age? She would promise me something but would fail to keep her word. To help ease the pain I began to tell myself that I hated her and I didn't want anything else to do with her. I thought hating her would be easier than the disappointment. I would write her and tell her stuff to hurt her feelings because I wanted her to feel the pain I was feeling. Every chance I got was another opportunity to hurt her. Still no one noticed how badly I was hurting.

I was so angry that I began to be rebellious. I was punching walls, screaming, and being very disrespectful. I didn't care about anything or anybody. Thinking back on it now, I took my anger out on my grandmother and she was the one taking care of me. She didn't have to take me in at all but she did and honestly, she did not deserve that. I pretty much gave her my butt to kiss and for that I am truly sorry. Now that I think about it, I was angry at the wrong person. I remember almost fighting my grandmother because I had so much built up anger that I had to release but I honestly didn't know how. I know now that everything that she did was to make me a better person, but back then I thought she was just being hard on me. All I wanted was my mother. I had a missing piece in my heart that I needed to be found.

The desire for my mom was becoming stronger every day. I even talked to my grandmother about discussing my desire to spend time with my mother, but my grandmother instructed me to leave it in the past. After I had that talk with my grandmother, I realized that I had to let it go.

About two years later, my mother was released and I, again, started to go visit her, I forgot about everything that made me angry and begin to think about what made me happy. I loved our one on one times together. We would walk along the beach and just talk until I had nothing else to say. Our one on one time was the best feeling in the world!

My mother had a very different way of parenting. She would allow my siblings and I to drink and smoke in front of her. She felt like she would rather us do it with her instead of in the streets. At that time it seemed cool. How many people could say that they had the opportunity to "turn up" with their mom? It was fun while it was going on, but I would have rather had a mother instead of a friend. I'm not saying she wasn't a mother, but I lacked the nurturing, support and guidance that I longed for.

I've often felt like the black sheep of the family. My

relationships with my siblings are nowhere close to what I feel it should be. They had the opportunity to form a close bond and I was robbed of that. I have known my brothers and sisters all of my life and I still feel as if I don' know them. I love each of them and I know they love me as well, however, our relationship is missing pieces that I feel my mother should have established between us, when she came home from prison.

I had to learn about womanhood on my own. No one taught me about a menstrual cycle, or what I was supposed to do when it started. I also had to learn what now comes with me having menstrual cycles. Those were things I looked to my mother to teach me, but she was not there. I had no one to teach me; not to mention how to be a mother to my own daughter.

I became responsible for a life when I could barely manage and maintain my own. Now, I hold my daughter so close to me because I never want her to experience what I had to live through. As her mother, I strive to be the best mother I can be regardless of what I didn't have. It took time, but I finally stopped dwelling on what I didn't have from my own mother and decided that I was no longer going to be angry and rather release her and extend forgiveness.

Now, this was no easy task. I had to be willing to take it moment by moment, step by step and day by day, while trusting and leaning on the Lord. Isaiah 1:18 says *"Come now, let us settle the matter,"* says the Lord. *"Though yours sins are like scarlet, they shall be as white as snow; though they are red as crimson, they shall be like wool."* My mother did what she thought was best for me and I learned that I couldn't keep holding her past over her head, yet wanting others to extend grace to me for my shortcomings. When someone hurts you all you want to do is return the feeling but, I encourage you to let go and let God. I know you will never forget what you have been through, but you have to accept that it did happen, find the lesson in it and move on. You will never move passed it if you keep holding on to it.

By now I'm sure the burning question within is: "How do I forgive?" For me, I prayed about my situation repeatedly and believed in God to heal me. I was so tired of hurting and being angry. My desire began as an act of faith. II Corinthians 5:17 reads: *"Therefore, if anyone is in Christ, he is a new creation; the old has gone, the new has come."* Everything my mother and I experienced was now gone and I had to make a decision to stop reliving it and the hurt every day of my life. Now, it was time to rebuild a relationship that had been broken for so many years.

When I was a freshman in high school I had a friend, we both shared the same name, she spelled hers with an "E". Shemeka and I connected instantly because we had similar life experiences and it was easy for us to relate to one another. She was a little bit older than me but she taught me how to forgive my mother. She also shared that although I would never forget what I went through I could no longer allow it to hold me captive; robbing me of my present life in which I couldn't enjoy due to failing to release pain from my childhood. Talking to my friend Shemeka, really helped me. She would encourage me to focus on the happy times I shared with my mom instead of reliving the painful moments.

It took me several years to actually release the hurt. Many of us talk about letting go, but truly letting go is a process. When I finally did, I was the happiest I had ever been. I was ready to start over and I did just that. I remember that day like it was yesterday. I came to Georgia a few weeks after I graduated from high school. I went straight to my mother's house. The first thing I did was hand her my diploma. This was one of the proudest moments for me because although she was unable to make it to my graduation, I still wanted to share that moment with her. I knew it was only by the grace of God that I even graduated from high school.

Once I showed my mom my diploma, that sparked a conversation and she began to share how she was so proud of me for finishing high school. She told me, *"You are 18 now, you can ask me anything that you want."* She felt I could finally handle the truth. As we were talking, I asked my mother the one burning question that I have been waiting for an answer to for many years; *Why did you give me to my grandmother?* My mother simply responded by saying, *"I knew that your grandmother could do a better job of raising you."* Hearing her answer caused me to cry. I cried but, they were not tears of sadness, but rather of release. It was the release I needed. I would never forget that day or discussion. It was at that very moment that I let go of the hurt, the anger, the pain, and the abandonment issues I was still carrying. I felt FREE! I was honestly tired of carrying it all. The weight of my abandonment was hard to carry. On that day I RELEASED IT!

My relationship with my mother may never be what I desire it to be and I have accepted that. She is in my life at this present time. Although we are not as close as I would like, the good thing is, she is still there. She could be completely absent. It's important that we learn to love our parents as they are and accept their weaknesses just as they accept ourselves. If you are facing what seems to be an endless battle with a loved one, I encourage you to never give up, never lose faith and believe that God can do anything!

Steps To Forgiveness

1. **Come to Terms-** Acknowledge the person that hurt you and how you felt when they did what they did to you.

2. **Forgive yourself-** Vow to yourself that you are going to do whatever you have to do to forgive so that you can begin healing.

3. **Ask Questions-** Find out why the person did what they did.

4. **Healthy Stress Relief-** Find healthy ways to relieve your stress from dealing with this situation. Some healthy stress relievers include:

    a) **Journaling.** Write down your thoughts and how it makes you feel.

    b) **Meditation.** Find you a quite area where you can be alone. Close your eyes and breathe in and out three time. On the third time hold that breathe in for about 5 seconds. Repeat if needed.

    c) **Finding a Hobby.** Do something that you enjoy. Enjoying your hobbies or even finding a new one is a great way to release stress.

I Forgive You

Mommy,

I hope this letter finds you in good health. All is well with Aniyah and I. . I know you are wondering why I'm writing you this letter and the reason being is because I have something to share with you. I know that you gave me to my grandmother because you couldn't take care of another child and I get that. I need you to understand that because of your decision to do that you hurt me more than you helped me.

I spent many nights in my room crying because of your decision.. I often asked, "Why me Lord?" Of all of her children to give away why did you choose me? I needed you more than you will ever know. Do you know that I would lock myself in my room at my grandmother's house and pretend to have a mother? I would sit there and talk to myself trying to imagine what it was to have a mother. The visits were cool but it wasn't enough for me. Honestly, I was so young I didn't know how to tell you I wanted more from you. I was very jealous and still am of the relationship that my siblings have with you.

I had to deal with the fact that you were in and out of my life and on top of that when you were released from prison you didn't come and get me. I found myself struggling as a parent because I didn't know how to be one. I never had you or my father in my life to teach me the essential things I needed to know. For so long I had so much hatred in my heart because I was hurting and felt like I couldn't talk to you about my feelings.

Mommy, I pray you understand why I had to get this out in order to move on with my life. Today I stand as a woman with many scars yet they no longer define or confine me. I am determined to move forward in the midst of all we have gone through. I know to increase our bond it will take tremendous efforts on both of our end however, I am committed to doing so. I also would like to let you know that I forgive you for the hurt you have caused in my life. Every tear I shed only allowed me to be in the place that I'm in now. I admit that although during the time it didn't feel good but it was all working for my good.

From this day forward I promise to never bring up the past anymore. All I want from you now is to first forgive me for the hurtful things I have said previously to intentionally hurt you. Secondly, I'd like for us to move past the hurt and the pain so that our relationship can become strengthened. I love you with all of my heart.

Sincerely yours,

Your Daughter

Chapter 2: Please Stop

Growing up I was bullied a lot by adults and children. I was a bowlegged skinny little girl that dressed like an old lady. When I went to school the children picked on me because of the clothes I wore. I didn't have name brand clothes or shoes, like my fellow classmates. My grandparents shopped at Walmart and thrift shops for my clothing. The children would befriend me just to be mean to me.

I can remember playing with my toys on the playground. Kids would ask me to hold my toys and I would let them. I actually thought that I was gaining new friendships, only to discover that they wanted my toys only to further pick and criticize me. They would take my toys and throw them on the ground. Sadly, before I could run to collect them, my teacher would always take them. I would never get them back.

Whenever this would happen, I would cry because I didn't understand why they did this to me. I was a very quiet child and didn't really talk much. I now realized that my peers used my quietness against me.

I was assigned a school friend. My school assigned "school friends" to those who were dealing with low self-esteem, bullying, and lack of social skills. The individual would come to the school, once a week, and literally be your friend. Mrs. Bobbi was my school friend. She was the sweetest woman I have ever met in my life. When I had bad days or was at my lowest, due to the constant bullying and put-downs from classmates, Mrs. Bobbi lifted my spirits. I wish I could find her and tell her thank you.

The children knew I didn't live with my mother so they would pick on me about living with my grandmother. They would say things like, "Dang your momma is old!" These were extremely hurtful, as they all knew that it was my grandmother and not my actual birth mother. Growing up, I heard so many hurtful words. My classmates would say I was ugly and my clothes came out of the garbage. While others laughed, I spent many days in tears.

I didn't have many people to speak into my life, but rather had many around me trying to tear me down. If the pressures of school weren't enough, I also had older people telling me I would end up pregnant and drop out of high school. I was often told that I would end up like my mother. This was my harsh reality. I now realize that most of the people that I was exposed to, at a young age, didn't have my best interest at heart.

I had very low self-esteem and value. Even when people tried to be positive, I rejected them. Someone could tell me I was pretty and I wouldn't believe them. I was indoctrinated into believing the negative things that were said to me year after year. I began to believe what others said about me. Due to the various pain and disappointments I experienced, I began not trust people when they said they loved me. Even to this day when people tell me they love me I find myself saying, "Do you really?" I admit I am working on this but it is still a process.

I never really spoke on being bullied because I felt that no one would listen. Would anyone even care? I can remember being told that they talked about Jesus and he made it through therefore, I would as well. I'd often hear, *"You're too soft Shameka."* or, *"Get a backbone Shameka."*

By nature I'm a loving and caring person. I'm always concerned about how others are feeling. All I truly wanted, as a child, was for someone to genuine love and care for me. I craved that daily. At a young age I felt like no one cared or loved me. I knew my grandparents loved me but I can count, on my hands, the number of times that they actually said it. No one will ever understand dealing with bullying alone. If I wasn't strong enough I probably would have tried to hurt myself or maybe even commit suicide, thank God for my strength.

After a while, I realized that enough was enough and I had to learn how to handle things differently. I grew tired of people running all over me and making me feel less than who I was and I begin to flip out. I told myself I would never get ran over again and I meant just that. I went from being that quiet, timid little girl to a rude, loud-mouth little girl. Whatever came to my mind was impulsively released. I would say exactly how I was feeling at the time to whomever and whenever. I began to think, *"Why should I care about your feelings when you don't care about mine?"*

After operating this way for a while I learned this wasn't the way to be either and honestly it wasn't showing others who I really was. I was allowing my pain to cause me to become just like those who had hurt me. I didn't want to be like those people.

From time to time, I admit that I may go from zero to a hundred real quick, but I have learned to ask God for a humble and calm spirit. I thank God for calming me down because at one point, I was completely out of control.

I could finally define myself. I knew who I wanted to be and I knew who I didn't want to be. I now thank the people who bullied me. Thank your bullies? Yes, I do! My bullies helped me to learn how to press through, regardless of what people say. They ignited my inner strength. Everything that was said to me, I now use as motivation. I strive to prove them wrong, by doing everything people once told me that I couldn't. I now know who I am because of them.

I am…………

* Beautifully and wonderfully made by God
* A Survivor
* Strong
* Caring
* Compassionate
* Stylish
* Determined
* Sweet
* Giving
* Smart
* Talented
* Kind
* Loving
* Humble
* Honest
* Hard- Working

When you are broken and you don't know who you are. Once you find true healing, you realize that everyone who told you that you were nothing and that you would never be good for anything, other than making babies, lied! I now know that I am who God says I am. I can do whatever God places within my hands to do.

I encourage you to write down every positive thought you have about yourself and put it on your mirror. Recite them daily until they are instilled in your mind and heart. My life coach gave me this assignment several years ago, when I couldn't think of anything positive about myself. In order to start, what felt like a very difficult assignment, she gave me the first five positive attributes and made me dig deep to find the rest. As I developed my list of self-affirmations, I realized that I had taken what others had said and made it my identity, when that wasn't who I was at all.

Sometimes you have to speak to yourself. Everyone is not going to always have your best interest at heart. They will love on you and beat you up, all in the same breath. Don't allow that to discourage you, but rather use it to become aware. We are all humans and subject to error. I now know that you do not have to accept what others say about you. Their opinions honestly do not have to matter unless you let them. Focus on becoming who

God has ordained you to be.

Another way for me to release or free myself from all of the hurt was through writing what I call "Letters of Release' to the different people who have hurt me. This exercise wasn't so much for them as it was for me. You see, I had to learn to be okay with the apology I may never receive. Sure this was hard and challenging, yet I had to get pass it for me. I wanted to be truly free and live in fullness.

Dear Bullies,

You will never know how much you damaged me as a child because you tore me down emotionally. You picked on me every day because I didn't look like you. Yes, my grandmother shopped at low budget stores for my clothing but did you know that she had the weight of her family on her shoulders? She provided me with what she could and I didn't have a problem with that.

Oh let me not forget about all the mean things you said to me that almost sent me over the edge. I sat in my bathroom many nights rocking back and forward feeling like I was about to lose my mind, not loving myself and contemplating on taking my own life. Back then I was weak so your words stuck in my head and I begin to think that what you were saying to and about me was true. Your words could have caused eternal damage but I made a decision to forgive you and denounce the negative words I had recited over my own life on account of you.

For too long I took your words for my own. The things you said almost became drilled into my head and for a while my actions became congruent with the words you spoke about me.
Until one day, I was reminded of who I really am in God. I was none of those things you said about me. I learned that I am precious in the eye sight of God and He created me before the foundation of the earth and I am not worthless but my life has meaning and I was placed here for a purpose.

Guess what else? I forgive you. I also took every negative word you ever spoke over me as motivation to live the best life I can on the earth. I graduated on time, didn't give birth to my daughter until I was twenty-one years old; nor did

I allow drugs to overtake my life. . Thank you for everything you said about me because you are part of the reason I am who I am today. I'm no longer tied to the hurt that you placed on my life. Like I stated I have forgiven you and I will no longer let what you did overtake my life or make me feel any hate for you. I'm released from you today. I speak blessings over you and pray that you are prospering wherever you are in all that you do.

Signed,

Your Victim ~ The Survivor

Chapter 3: Silent Tears

Silent tears were something I knew oh too well. For many years, as a child, I was a victim of molestation by people that were close to my family. I knew that it was not supposed to be happening, but I was too afraid to tell anyone. One of the individuals even threatened me that if I told anyone he would tell everyone it was me that was touching him and everyone would believe him. I felt as if it was pointless to mention it to my family because I didn't feel like they would believe me.

I had a very close knit family and at the time I honestly felt that if I said anything it would be dismissed or swept under the rug, so I dared to ever mention again. I will never understand why these individuals did this to me, but I'm glad it was me and not any of my other little cousins. I was their refuge. My hurt, heartache and brokenness kept them safe and for at least that, I am grateful. The hardest part was facing that fact that those who should of loved and protected me, actually did not truly love me. They were my violators.

As I grew up, my violation haunted me. Due to my molestation, I had to deal with the urge and desire to have sexual encounters. The desire to have the physical feeling became stronger. At a young and vulnerable age, I was already aware of the feeling; that rush through my body when I was touched and I wanted more. Sadly, I wouldn't have known or even desired sex so early if I wasn't molested.

I began to have sex at the age of fourteen. I felt like boys loved me so I freely began having sex with my 'boyfriends'. I remember thinking I was grown and had it all figured out. One day I snuck out and picked up some birth control; it only got worst from there. I didn't have anybody to tell me the consequences of having sex. At fourteen, I was learning on my own or through friends, books, and sexual education. Once I started I couldn't stop. I was sleeping with different people and unprotected. From one-night stands to meeting guys on dating websites and having sex with them, I loved sex and it made me feel like I was someone. I equated sex to love and I deserved to be loved!

In my search for real love vs physical passion, I even had a few pregnancy scares. I will never forget the time I was living across the street from a college university and my friend, at the time, and I liked to hang out at the college. As we were still young, we were not allowed to go to the college, but would lie about our whereabouts. My girlfriend and I would go to the college for parties, probates, and to hang out in the dorms.

One particular day, we were on campus visiting two guy friends that we always kicked it with, but this day was different. For some reason, my girlfriend went to one of the guy's rooms and I ended up going to the other. At first it was cool. We listened to music and ate pizza. Then things changed and I was no longer comfortable. The guy began to feel on me and kiss me, but I didn't want him to, because I was in a committed relationship. I asked him to stop, but he didn't. He began taking off my clothes and while he was holding me down he inserted himself into me. As tears rolled down my face I remember begging him to stop, as I declared aloud the love for my boyfriend. He stopped.

My boyfriend was cool with me having guy friends because he trust me enough to know that I would never do anything to hinder our relationship. Before that day the guy and I were never alone in the dorm together. When I think back on it, even when I realized that we were alone together, I wasn't worried because he was the Homie; at least that's what I thought. Now I know better.

Even if you know an individual, you must look for and be careful of the signs and signals. Those they give off and the ones that you give off to them; especially when you are alone. In his mind, he thought, "she wants to have sex with me". He probably thought that because I didn't voice that I didn't feel comfortable being alone with him, or ask that we all hang out together. He probably thought my silence what an open invitation for sex, it wasn't. While I acknowledge my silence, nothing gave him the right to rape me. When I did become vocal and shout for him to stop, he should of.

Eventually he stopped, I got dressed and went home. I cried to one of my family members, but she brushed it off. She was more upset at the fact that I lied about where I was going, than me being sexually violated and raped! I remember leaving her bedroom feeling worthless. I was so disgusted with myself and the decisions I had made. Did I bring this on myself? Did I deserve what had happened to me? Truth is, no I shouldn't have been in another guy's dorm room especially if I had a boyfriend. However, no one deserves to be raped. No one!

Due to his forceful efforts, I was in a lot of pain. I decided to sit in the tub and cleanse my body of what had happened. As I sat in the tub, the tears rolled down my face. I couldn't believe this had just happened to me. I could recall all of the times I thought I was untouchable and nothing would ever happen to me, but in that very moment I realized it wasn't true. The reality of the situation hit me all at once. I realized that I could of very well lost my life that night.

That night pushed me into a depression. I was empty inside. I felt unclean and broken. I remember blaming myself for this encounter, because I shouldn't have been over there in the first place. This was truly an expensive lesson I had to learn.
Word of advice, when your parents or anyone close to you, tell you not to do something it's not because they are trying to ruin your life or fun. It's because they are trying to protect you from hurt. Listen to what they are saying because that could easily be the one thing that can save your life. They have been there and only want the very best for you.

After experiencing that moment, it changed my life forever. I struggled in various relationships. I felt damaged and didn't know how to properly deal with the pain, anger and embarrassment. I dealt with infidelity in my relationships, because the guy I later dated felt I was not properly catering to his sexual needs. After being raped, I didn't want anyone to touch me, not even my boyfriend. My hurt closed the world out and my relationship suffered the most. I wasn't myself and because we were young, we didn't really know how to handle such an adult situation. Sadly, my boyfriend didn't confess his infidelity; I learned this information from his mom. This was definitely a slap in my face. I remember feeling so heartbroken and disappointed. Everywhere I turned people I loved were disappointing and hurting me. I ended up spending a lot of time in my room crying. It often felt as if no one cared or felt my pain. On the bright side of things I didn't end up pregnant or with an STD. I guess that was something to celebrate huh?

Throughout this long process of healing, I am proud to say that I have learned to love myself again. I began with this scripture Jeremiah 6:14, *"They have healed also the hurt of the daughter of my people slightly, saying, Peace, Peace; when there is no peace."* I will never forget that it happened to me, but I had to be freed from those situations. People ask me how I'm able to be around one of the individuals that molested me. I see them from time to time when I go home. My response is, *"By the grace of God."*

I can remember attending a church service and receiving a word directly from the pastor, who identified me in the audience, his message literally changed my life. He told me that every hurt I had experienced in my life was going away, but it depends on how bad I wanted it. I praised God like never before! I cried, screamed, shouted, and ran all around that church. That night, I felt as if the weight of the world was lifted off of my shoulders.

Next, I prayed and asked God to restore me. I wanted him to show me who I was in His eyes. I continued to pray this prayer and grow closer to God daily. My faith increased. Lastly, I had to speak life to myself. I had to let myself know that I was beautifully and wonderfully made in the sight of God. No matter what I went through, God didn't allow me to look like what I had been through. If I had to leave anything with you I would simply say that you are so much stronger than what you realize. God has gifted you with an extraordinary internal strength to get through whatever you are facing. God won't let it take you under! How do I know? Because I made it through and I am still here! If God did it for me, He will do it for you. Whatever you are facing will become your testimony, to help someone else heal from the very thing that had once caused you the most pain.

During the process of healing it is important to be honest with God about the way you feel and were affected by whatever has taken place in your life. This part is not always pretty, but necessary! You must then be willing to forgive yourself, the other individual(s) and God. Often times we get upset with God and blame Him for allowing certain things to happen to us, but in the end it all works together for our good (Romans 8:28.)

If you are in need of prayer, for any of the things I have mentioned above, receive this prayer as a token of my love for you:

Pray this prayer aloud:

"Lord, I come to you as humbly as I know how. I ask you to cover the individual that is dealing with rape or molestation. Wrap your loving arms around them and let them know that you are right there. Release them from the embarrassment, guilt or hurt. Let them know that it was NOT their fault. Help them to forgive the person who has sinned against them and know that vengeance is not theirs, but unto the Lord. Let them know that every tear that they have shed was a liquid prayer that you have heard. Lord, touch their minds and help them to understand that you would not put any more on them than they are able to bear. Heal them right now Lord. Deliver them right now. Restore them right now. In Jesus name we pray, Amen."

Regardless of what you have been through, know that healing is possible! It is not always easy, but trust God and trust the process. Walk forward in your life, knowing that you will be okay. Today, I decree and declare that once you are released from this bondage, you are going to your NEXT LEVEL!

Dear Molester,

    You took something from me that I will never be able to get back and that was my innocents. As a little girl I replayed you touching me over and over again in my head. Why me? What pleasure did you get by touching me? I knew what you did to me wasn't right, but who would believe me? I can hear my family now telling me it's just my imagination or I'm making up stories so I held it in.

    I'm writing you this letter today, to let you know that I have reclaimed my life back and I forgive you. I can never forget what happen, but in order for me to be all God would have me to be, I had to find it within myself to forgive you. You taught me that you cannot have your children around everyone, because what you did to me could happen to anybody.

    Now that I have a daughter, I guard her with my whole heart because I had no one protecting me from the monster that you were. My prayer is that you find forgiveness for your own self-healing as well as getting the help you need.

Signed,

The Reclaimer

Chapter 4: My Best Friend

I honestly don't know where to begin when it comes to my grandfather. All I can say is that he was the best thing that ever walked into my life. The bond that my grandfather and I share was unbreakable. I don't think anyone could come in between us, if they tried. Granddaddy was my protector and I was his Meka-Moe.

When I was sick, he was there. When I was sad, he was there. He made sure no one hurt me. I can remember when my grandma used to spank me, I would scream so loud that my granddaddy would come out of his room and fuss at her. My grandmother would get so upset with me for doing that because she knew that beating session was over. Granddaddy didn't care if I was right or wrong, he didn't want her or anyone bothering me.

Let me tell you how serious our relationship was. My grandfather brought a mini refrigerator and placed it in his room so that I could store my favorite snacks in his room because my grandmother didn't allow me to drink soda and eat a lot of snacks. I never told her and neither did he.

This man treated me like I was his very own. Never did I feel like he was my grandfather. I felt like he was my daddy. He was the only man I knew. He showed me how I should be treated. My grandfather always made it happen for me. If I wanted my nails done he would pay for me to get it done every two weeks. I remember wanting to learn how to drive and he tried to teach me, but I hit a tree. (It's okay you can laugh.) I was a terrible driver and I believe that was the first time I heard my Granddaddy tell me anything negative. When it came to driving that became off limits. When I go back home to visit I still laugh because that same tree is still there, still leaning.

I will never forget the day I wanted pizza and my grandmother told me no. My granddaddy got up and got dressed and went to get my pizza! On his way back home, as my grandfather was turning onto our road, someone hit him and he had to go to the hospital. Now you can imagine what I was thinking... this was all my fault because I just had to have pizza. I was so upset. Luckily, granddaddy ending up being okay and guess what else? Even as they were attempting to transport him to the hospital, he made sure he got me that pizza! Now that is love.

When I moved to North Carolina our bond remained close. We never missed a beat in each other's lives. Then the unthinkable happened. My grandfather suddenly became ill. He was sicker than I thought. Everyone always kept things from me because they said I'm too sensitive. I knew something wasn't right because my granddaddy never missed my birthday and that particular year, he didn't call. I ended up calling him and he said he forgot. I knew then that things would never be the same. I had to get home to see him, but there was only problem, I wasn't working and I didn't have the money to do so. I cried many nights because I needed to get home to see him. When I talked to him on the phone, I would tell him that I would get home to see him soon and take care of him when I got there. A month or so went by and I still hadn't made it home.

One night I returned home from the grocery store and received a call from my grandmother. My grandmother wanted me to come home and that I needed to get on the first train there. I wasn't prepared, so I asked her could I just come the next day. She insisted that I come that night. Something was not right and I had no idea what it was.

I got on the next train heading to Georgia. Those were the longest six hours of my life. My head was spinning because I didn't know what I was getting ready to walk into. While I was on the train, I called my granddaddy and I told him I was on the way and that I loved him. I arrived to Georgia and my aunt was waiting there to pick me up. She told me that we needed to head straight to the hospital, which was about a forty-five minute drive from the train station. Along the way I insisted that we stop at a convenient store so I could get a charger for my phone. After doing so, we continued on to the hospital.

When we arrived, I felt butterflies in my stomach, as I walked towards the ICU unit. My grandmother met us at the door with her face full of tears. In my twenty-one years of life, I had never seen my grandmother cry. She didn't have to say anything, because I already knew. As I threw my glasses across the room, tears filled my face. All I could utter was, "NO! I didn't get to see him before he died." My grandmother finally told me that my grandfather died twenty minutes before I arrived. If only I didn't stop for my charger, I would have made it to say my final goodbye. I silently sat in the waiting room, crying and waiting for the rest of my family to get there. I had to be the one to let everyone know that he passed away because my grandmother couldn't get her words together. The doctor asked the family to go back and view his body. I couldn't do it.

Everyone came out crying and we left.

As we prepared for my granddaddy's funeral, I just couldn't seem to get it together. Visitors were coming in and out and I knew I had to be there for my grandmother, but I too had a hole in my heart. My heart was broken because I had just lost my best friend, protector and confidante. What was I going to do now? My grandfather was my biggest cheerleader. He was the father I never had. Silent tears are something I know too well. For many months, I cried myself to sleep. If I may be quite honest with you, I'm still trying to cope and it's been 9 years since his passing.

Dealing with grief is similar to dealing with abuse, they both are never easy to overcome and require you to go through all the stages. It is truly a process, but I can actually say that I am doing a whole lot better than what I was a few years ago. I cope with my grandfather's loss by focusing on the blessings of his life. I remember all the positive things that we did instead of only focusing on how much I miss him. This was the hardest chapter for me to write, because I miss him so much. Now, whenever I return home, I want to visit his grave to fully get closure, but my grandmother is not ready yet and I have to respect that. I don't really stay at my grandmother's house too often, because it brings back too many memories for me.

Another way I've learned to cope is by telling my daughter about how great of a person my grandfather was. There is not a day that goes by that I don't think about him. I used to sit and cry, but now I reminisce and laugh at all the crazy things we did together. I find joy in that.

If you currently grieving the lost of a loved one who passed either recently or some time ago, I encourage you to find someone that you can trust and express your feelings to them. If you have to cry it's okay, let it out. The worst thing that you can do is keep your grief bottled up. Letting the tears flow is a form of release and it will help ease the hurt and pain. Focus on the blessings of their life; the things your loved one or friend enjoyed doing. Take time to look at old pictures and instead of getting angry, smile and laugh. Never allow anyone to tell you that you need to get over it. Everyone grieves differently and at their own pace. While you are never truly over it, you learn to find ways to count the blessings and find your joy after your loss. Take as long as you need, but remember they are truly in a better place and God's will you will see them again.

Dear Granddaddy,

I still haven't been able to get past the reality of not being able to see you before your transition. I know I talked to you a few hours before you passed, but that was not enough for me. When I loss you, I lost a part of myself. Nobody will ever understand our relationship. It was truly special and one I will cherish forever. You taught me how to love and how to be okay not having everyone's support as long as I received it from those who mattered most.

You taught me how to cook and gave me my first driving lesson. I'm laughing right now because that tree I hit is still leaning. Granddaddy, you teased me for a long time about that and you laughed at me because my legs were shaking uncontrollably. We had so much fun together! I remember when you brought me all those shrimp and I ate until I got so sick that I told you, "I am never eating shrimp again!" You already knew that was a lie. We truly had some great times.

I promise to take care of grandma for you. She is still fussing as usual. She always tells me that she wishes you had the opportunity to meet your great granddaughter, Aniyah. I found out that I was expecting a month after you transitioned. I wish you were here to meet her because I know you would love her just as much as you loved me.

Grandaddy, since you are gone, I have no reason to go home. Grandma comes up here a lot, so I do get to see her. I miss you more than you will ever know, but I know you are at peace now. I love you so much.

Signed,

"Meka- Moe"

Chapter 5: I Can Smile Again

A month after I buried my grandfather I got sick. I woke up feeling horrible, so I asked my boyfriend to go with me to the hospital. I was in so much pain I could have cried. We arrived at the hospital and after a long wait, that literally felt like it took forever, I eventually got called to the back. The doctor came in and asked me what was going on and I recall telling her and she asked me was there any way I could be pregnant. My response was, "Absolutely not!" I was confident in my answer because I had just taken a pregnancy test a week ago and it was negative. They continued to run several test and came back in the room to confirm that I indeed was pregnant!

I was in total shock! My boyfriend was super excited and screaming, " I told you so!" I didn't want to hear anything he had to say because we argued the whole ride to the hospital on whether or not I was really expecting. I wanted to be happy, but I knew this was about to be a struggle for both of us because neither of us were employed. The way we pictured the both of us reacting to the news of us becoming parents was completely opposite of what actually happen. We knew that our very lives were about to change in a drastic way.

Although he assured me everything was fine, a week after I found out I was pregnant, my boyfriend left town. He said he needed time to wrap his mind around being a parent. I was heartbroken. I had just found out I was pregnant and he left. I remember wanting to abort my baby because I didn't want to continue this journey alone. I was twenty-one and he was eighteen; so we were still babies ourselves.

I went to my second doctor's appointment and what I thought was going to be a good appointment turned out to be an ultimate scare. I had to receive an ultrasound and learned that my daughter had an irregular heartbeat. I was then transferred to a high-risk clinic to have more tests. Unfortunately the tests confirmed the worst. The doctors told me my daughter would need open-heart surgery performed on her as soon as she was born. I remember leaving my appointment definitely prepared to have an abortion. Not only did I have to deal with possibly raising this child alone, but now to learn that she would need surgery was all too much for me.

One day, while I was on the bus going home, I called my boyfriend's mother to share the news from the appointment. She prayed for me as well as my baby and encouraged me that everything was going to be ok.

As I was searching through the yellow pages something happened that immediately captured my attention and shifted my focus. Out of the blue I felt my baby kick! It was too soon for my baby to be kicking but it happened just one time. At that very moment I knew I could no longer abort my baby. The bond between this unborn vessel now appeared precious in my eyesight. It's amazing how even from the wound my daughter had a positive effect on my life. I remember growing up being the baby and now I was pregnant with a little person I was responsible for raising.

I remember having extreme anger issues as a child, which followed me into my adulthood. Once I found out I was pregnant, my temperament changed. I calmed down, as I quickly realized that things would no longer be all about me anymore. She also taught me that everyone doesn't have your best interest at heart. Throughout my whole pregnancy I learned so much about myself as well as things I need to get right before my daughter was born.

The closer I got to my due date, the more excited I got because my life was getting ready to change in a good way. The day that my daughter entered this world started off with a simple doctor's appointment that quickly turned into them inducing my labor! My blood pressure was high and my baby was hooked up to the monitor but she wasn't making too much movement. My water had been leaking, so there was very little amniotic fluid around her. I was extremely nervous as I didn't know what to expect. I didn't want anything to happen to my baby nor did I want anything to happen to me. As I was being transferred to the maternity unit, I called my pastor's wife and close family, to inform them on the change in my situation and the need to induce my labor. My family and friends began to arrive to show their love and support.

As my blood pressure escalated, I wanted to be excited but I was so sick. At that point I was just ready for it to be over. Through all the pain, when I gave birth to my daughter it was the most beautiful moment of my life; one that I will forever cherish. As I held her I began to speak over her life.

I began to declare:
You are healed. You are purpose-filled.
You will never lack. You will succeed in life.
You are anointed. You are destined for greatness.

I did this because growing up many spoke negatively over my life and I wanted my voice to be the first my daughter heard declaring what God's word says about her, over her.

The day she was born was the day my daughter's father and I decided we were going to try to make things work for our baby. My daughter's father supported me through my whole pregnancy. We just decided, earlier in my pregnancy, that we wouldn't be in a relationship. During our nine-month break, we had time to work on the issues that caused so many problems in our relationship. Who knew that someone so small could mend relationships and make someone so happy. We named our precious daughter Aniyah.

Aniyah taught me how to truly love again. I had been hurt so many times in my life that I felt like I didn't know what true love was, but as soon as I pushed her out, I was instantly in love. She opened up my eyes and I have never felt this type of love before March 12, 2009. My love for Aniyah was unconditional. It was God's gift. From that day on, my life has to never been the same.

Once Aniyah was born, she motivated me to do and become better. Before I became a mother, I used to get mad and wanted to fight. Now, I think about the consequences of beating people up. When I wanted to quit my job, my daughter reminded me that I couldn't take care of her if I didn't work. She motivated me to calm down and think before I would act.

A lot of people think you cannot learn from your children, but you actually can. My daughter has taught me about this thing called life. I only want the best for my daughter. I want her to be and do whatever her heart desires. I want her to never allow anyone or anything to tear her down or make her lose sight of her self-worth.

If I had to leave a nugget for young mothers it would simply be this: Motherhood is not the end of your life. You can achieve all your dreams in the midst of raising your child(ren.) It may take a little longer to accomplish but you can do it. People are going to have negative things to say, but let it roll off of your shoulders. Your child is not a mistake. God blessed you to be a mother for a reason. I encourage you to be the best mother you can be. Also, just because you have a baby by a man doesn't mean you two are meant to be together or make it work for the baby's sake. Your child deserves to be raised in a healthy and peaceful environment, whether that means a one-parent or two-parent home. I tried to stay with my boyfriend but found that it only made things worst. If you are unhappy, as a couple, don't stay. It will only make you an unhappy mother.

Here are a few affirmations for mothers. Declare these over your life daily:

I AM……

A great mother

A motivator

A provider

I'm patient

I listen to the heart of my child

I deserve the best

My child deserves the best

I love my child just the way he or she is

All good things are coming to me

I'm strong

WE are going to make it

Dear Aniyah,

The day you were born was the best day of my life. You taught me what true love was. When I gave birth to you I was clueless on how to be a mother, but I did my very best. All I wanted was to give you what I didn't have growing up.

I'd like to apologize to you for any situations you had to experience at such a young age. I apologize for not giving you a stable living environment and for not being able to feed you much at sometimes. Only your father and I knew how many nights we went to bed with no food only to ensure you ate. As your mother it is my job to never let you go hungry.

The great thing about this process is we are learning together and I thank you for being patient with me. I also would like for you to know that it was you who saved my life. There were times that I wanted to give up, but because of you, I dusted myself off and kept pressing forward. I tell you all of the time that you are my lifeline and I truly mean it. If God didn't bless me with you, I honestly don't know where I will be. Thank you for being the best daughter anyone could ask for. When I can't pray for myself you were always right there praying for me. You cover me as well as I cover you and for that I am forever grateful.

I promise to always be here for you. I will never leave your side and vow to support you in everything you desire to do in life. Know that you are destined to be great and you can do anything you set your mind to. Never let anyone ever tell you differently. I love you and thank you for being my heartbeat. I love you so much.

Signed,
Your Mother

Chapter 6:
My Bittersweet Love Story

One Sunday while I was in service, I connected with a guy that was sitting in the musician section at my church. Can I be honest with you? I had a thing for musicians. After service, this particular day, the musician approached me. While I knew that he was trying to get my attention, I did what most girls do; I acted uninterested. The musician left me alone. The following Sunday, I came to church to find one of the young ladies that I mentor covered with hickeys all over her neck. Shocked, I asked her where they came from. She surprisingly told me it was that same musician.

After that discovery, I knew there was no way I could talk to him. Later in the service, the musician tried to talk to me again. I walked right by him, as if I didn't even see him. The next time I saw him was during bible study and he followed me to my roommate's car. He was very persistent and three years younger than me. I was twenty and he was only seventeen and was still in high school. Now, I'm not going to lie, I enjoyed the chase! He was very persistent in trying to win my heart but it still was not good enough.

That night, once my roommates and I arrived back home, the musician became the topic of our late-night discussion. My roommates began to share their opinions on the situation. They thought he was way too young for me. One even asked me, *"How dare you consider dealing with someone who was trying to pursue a young lady that you mentored?"* My roommates shared their fear that someone, in this situation, would get hurt. I'm sure, as you read this, you may be thinking the exact same thing but, I was blinded by my brokenness. Although I had people warning me, I totally went against all of their advice. Something within me desired him and honestly I wanted him even more as they continued to share all of the reasons why I shouldn't pursue it.

No one knew we had exchanged numbers that night. No one had a clue that I would lie alone in my bed, talking to him on the phone for hours! The conversation was great. The musician and I continued to talk daily for a few weeks before we decided to make it official. We began to contemplate when we were going to tell everyone that we were together. We first had to prepare for the negative comments we were going to receive because we decided to be in a relationship. The next day we attended a birthday party for one of our mutual friends. He introduced me to his mom and everything else was history. Every time you saw him, you saw me and every time you saw me, he wasn't far behind. We were truly inseparable. Things were going great. I went on his family trips and travel with his mother to minister in various cities. We grew close rather quickly. Once we begin to have intercourse, it seemed like we grew even closer than before.

We used to always talk about the future. He would always tell me that he wanted us to have a family together and we were going to get married. I believed everything he told me because I loved him and I had no reason not to believe him. I ended up quitting my good paying job just to lay up with him all day. Believe it or not we would try quite often.

The moment I found out I was pregnant everything changed. A week after we found out I was pregnant he left to go to New York because he had to wrap his mind around that fact that he was about to be a daddy. That's when I realized promises can be broken. When he finally decided to come back we were no longer in a relationship. It just wasn't working out for us. He wanted to run the streets and smoke instead of being in a relationship with me. He was not focused, as I was, on preparing for our baby. I felt so stupid because I believed all the things he told me and now here I was stuck with no job, no man, and a baby.

After I gave birth to my daughter I ended up finding a job. I began working at a county jail in the kitchen and this is where I met my new boo. Again, he was a person everyone told me not to go with, but I didn't listen. I saw something in him that no one else did and I gave him a chance. (This seemed to be a pattern with me.) He was one of the sweetest people I had ever met. We had dated for a few weeks and saw each other while my daughter visited her father on the weekends. I would go and stay with him until my daughter returned. Everything was great between us. I would go home and get more clothes and by the time I got back he would already have had dinner made.

One particular evening my daughter's father ended up sending a text message apologizing for everything he put us through. He wanted a second chance. Now, although I was in a new relationship, my daughter's father was the love of my life. I was willing to leave my current boyfriend for my daughter's father because he really completed me. For us it was more than just make it work for our daughter, we genuinely balanced each other out. I ended up calling my current boyfriend over to my house so that we could talk. He came over and I told him that my daughter's father and I decided to work things out. I could see the hurt and disappointment all over his face. I felt like the most horrible person it the world. To make matters worse, he and I were coworkers, so when I returned to work, the next day, it was extremely awkward. Tension at work continued to grow. I would overhear him having conversations about how stupid he felt I was for going back to my daughter's father. It hurt my heart to hear those things because it was never my intention to hurt him. I just loved my daughter's father a little bit more. We had deep history. When everything in life was going wrong he was there. He knew the right words to say to put the biggest smile on my face. I loved the bond that we shared. We were the true definition of *Ride or Die*.

Everything was going great between my daughter's father and I. We decided to move in together, as a family, and began looking at apartments. I was approved for the apartment and it brought me back to the reality of our situation. I remember being so happy and unable to believe this was actually happening! At this point my daughter's father had dropped out of high school and was supposed to be in the process of looking for a job, so he couldn't contribute and the financial responsibility was on me.

We moved into our little one bedroom apartment. While it wasn't much, it was ours. Our living situation was good initially. I was working and he was a stay-at-home dad, but that grew old real quick! I was working my butt off every day and he was sitting at home, getting high all day, and doing the bare minimum to help financially. So many times I'd come home and he would have a house full of guys in my home getting high. After a while, I too became drawn into this vicious cycle and would spend my last dime on Marijuana. We were also real close to our neighbors therefore, we would spend many nights outside smoking and drinking with them talking about life issues and our relationship problems. I felt like our relationship was nothing more than us getting high and having sex all day, every day. Don't get me wrong, we had some great days, but realistically our bad outweighed our good.

One day I got sent home from work early because I got into fist-fight with a male supervisor in the kitchen of the jail. Another supervisor had to come break us up. I was instructed to leave and was threatened with arrest. I did as I was instructed to do and prepared to head home. I returned home and shared my news with my boyfriend. Naturally, he was upset that another man put their hands on me and wanted to fight him as well. I explained to him that it wasn't worth neither of our freedom so he left it alone. Needless to say this particular day was not a good day. I was worried that I would be fired for my actions. My boyfriend had his own life issues going on. So we decided that we were going to forget about our issues and try to enjoy the rest of our day. My boyfriend went on a store run while I was home preparing for us to smoke. Once my boyfriend came back from the store their was a lot of smoking and drinking for the majority of the day.

Later that night, we got into this big argument and he told me how he really felt. He told me it was my fault I got in that fight at work earlier that day and that I'm always complaining. He went on to share that I don't spend enough time with our daughter because I'm always sleeping. My boyfriend's words angered me and I flipped. I went into the kitchen pulled out a knife and tried to cut him. All the built-up frustration was coming out at this very moment. How dare he question anything that I did when I was the one waking up at 3am to be at work at 4am. I was the one ensuring that we had a place to stay and food to eat. I don't spend much time with our daughter because I was tired. I come home take a nap, cook, do homework, spend time with my daughter, and smoke with him every day. That was our daily routine.

My boyfriend ended up calling his mom to tell her what happened. As a grandmother, his mother's main concern was our daughter and removing her from this hostile situation. She told us that we needed to work it out on our own. Our daughter left with her grandmother and not too long after that, my boyfriend followed. He never came back home that night. I cried and cried all night. Why did this happen? This relationship was becoming unhealthy for me. I was never this angry before we moved in together. Now, I was always angry. I felt the weight of the world on my shoulders and just needed some help. The next morning he came back home. We apologized to each other and immediately fell back into our unhealthy cycle, smoking and having sex. When things went wrong in our relationship we always went to marijuana, alcohol, and sex because to us, that numbed the hurt and frustration. That made everything better.

After we had our first big blow, we decided that we were just going to leave it in the past. We were unhappy together, but we loved each other too much to let go of our unhealthy relationship. In our relationship we didn't deal with the issues, we let the drugs ease our pain. I would find myself so high and drunk in the middle of the day just so I wouldn't have to deal with the things that we were going through. We would start early in the morning and wouldn't stop until we passed out. I begin to lose sight of what was important and that's when our bills begin to get behind. I wasn't making enough money to pay the bills and support our habits.

For a brief moment, we were able to catch up because my boyfriend found a job. He was working in the heat between 8 to 10 hours a day and one day he got really sick and quit. We were determined that we were going to make it somehow. I can't really explain our thought process, but clearly it wasn't to smart. We attempted to sell marijuana but we smoked more of our product than we actually sold. Things for us just never seem to get back on track. Our lease was about to end and we had no idea where we were going. We didn't have any money. He didn't want to go back home and neither did I.

Moving day finally came and we had nowhere to go. We put everything that we owned in storage, except our clothes. When it was late at night we would go sleep in our old apartment. We never turned the keys in to the management office because we needed somewhere to stay. At this time, my daughter was with her grandmother, so we knew that she would be taken care of until we found a place. One of my friends told us that we could move in with her and we did, for a few days, but it didn't work out. I cherished our friendship more than us living together so I moved before our friendship was ruined.

We ended up moving into my aunt's house for a while. In the beginning it was cool, but then my aunt's boyfriend didn't like that my boyfriend was staying there so he told her that he had to find somewhere else to live. I fought hard for my family, so if my boyfriend had to go, we all did. I searched until I found us another place. Now, we could get out of my aunt house. We moved into a two-bedroom house. God had given us a second chance. This move made me realize that it was time for us to really get our lives together.

I was so excited for the move. My excitement quickly faded when I found out that I only lived two houses down from my ex, the one that I ended things with to get back with my boyfriend. Things couldn't have gotten any more awkward then at that very moment. It was already hard enough seeing him everyday at work. I just knew it was going to be problems, but it actually turned out not to be so bad. My ex and boyfriend actually started hanging together.

One day, as we were sitting outside smoking, my boyfriend and I decided that this was our house to make things better. We made a promise to each other that there wouldn't be anymore fighting and he would find a job. He was determined that he was going to keep his promise to me, so each day after I came home from work he would leave to go job hunting. All his hard work finally paid off and he found a job. I was so happy that things were really beginning to look up for us. Our arguments ended, as our work schedules did not afford us a lot of time to see each other. The time apart made us grow closer because we missed each other. From time-to-time, we had our struggles, but we always found a way to get out of it. I could remember one time when we didn't have anything to eat in our house and the only money we had was the rent money. My boyfriend went to donate his blood plasma to feed his family. On the way to the clinic, he was stopped by the police and was arrested. He had a previous warrant from years back.

At the time, I was working at the jail, so I walked by the holding cells not even knowing that he was in one of them! I went and picked up my daughter from daycare and went home. I was still trying to figure out what we were going to eat. Later that afternoon, I received a phone call from the County Jail. It was my boyfriend telling me he had been arrested. I couldn't believe it. He told me that need needed $150 to be released. All the money I had was the rent money, so we decided that we wouldn't touch that. My aunt ended up calling me to ask a question and I asked her to borrow the money. I dropped my daughter off, at her home, and I went to meet the bail bondmen. This was one of the scariest things I had to do. It was dark and I had to meet him a few blocks away from the jail. I paid the bail money and sat waiting for his release.

When he saw, me he ran and picked me up and gave me the biggest hug and kiss ever. As we exited the jail, I lit a cigarette and gave it to him because I knew he needed it. He stopped in the middle of the street to check his wallet. When he looked inside, he was shocked to find that the police didn't find the weed that he had stashed. He was incredibly lucky! We actually still laugh about that to this day. We walked to pick up our daughter from my aunt's. My aunt gave us some food to cook for the night and we journeyed home. That night, my boyfriend told me that I was a true definition of a *Ride or Die* girlfriend because I stopped everything that I was doing to go and rescue him. I expressed my love for him and shared that I would do anything for him.

After that, things got back to normal. Then, I began to notice that my boyfriend started staying up late and was acting funny. One day I did the unthinkable and went through his phone. Now, I was always told to never go searching because you will find just what you are looking for and I did. I went through his phone and saw that he had been talking to this girl that lived by my aunt house. I sent the girl a text messaged, telling her to stop texting my boyfriend. I'm assuming she told him that I contacted her because he flipped.

At first it was just arguing and then it got physical. He was pushing me around our living room. I was fighting back the whole time. I felt bad because our daughter was right there crying. I wasn't even hurt that he pushed me, I was more upset that he was trying to play me. I'm sitting here taking care of him and this was how he was going to repay me! While we were fighting, I was constantly screaming my hate and frustration at him, "*I hate you. I wish I never met you. You are so stupid.*" All of my anger came rushing out. We managed to calm down.

The girl called him and said she wanted to meet me and talk. He was so scared to invite her over because he knew I was a little on the crazy side. I agree to meet and talk, but I also called my cousin over to make sure to keep me calm throughout the confrontation. This was at a point in my life that I would go from 0 to 100 real quick. The girl came over and we talked and smoked and it was cool. There seemed to be nothing going on, so I dropped it, but it seemed like once we would get over one thing, something else would happen.

One day when we came home my family had no water. The water company said we were tampering with the box, which wasn't true. So they wouldn't restore our water. We took baths at my aunt house and our neighbor let us use his water to cook and use the bathroom. My aunt's boyfriend went and discussed our situation with family members that ran my name through the dirt. Everything in my life was falling apart. I can't remember why, but my boyfriend and I ended up getting into another fight not too long after. This fight was the fight that ended us.

I remember our house looking like a tornado had hit. This physical altercation was real. I would hit him and he would hit me right back. I tried to call the police, but he took my phone and threw it. He had me pinned down so I couldn't move. The whole time, I'm kicking him as hard as I can. This fight shook me and I knew that we were not coming back from this one. The next day, I sat him down and told him that we needed a break to get our lives together. I told him that I was taking our daughter and going back to Georgia. He said he thought it was best and while we were gone he was going to make himself better. It was time for me to get out. I knew I had to leave.

If you have ever been or are in an unhealthy or abusive relationship, I encourage you to get help or leave too. You never want to be in a situation where it becomes abusive and your children see it. My daughter is nine years old and she is still affected by what she has seen happen in front of her. Abuse doesn't just affect the one being hit, but everyone in the family.

There are no excuses for abuse and everyone needs to seek counseling and you must find a way to exit the unhealthy relationship. Your life and the lives of your children depend on it.

In Ecclesiastes 3:1 it reads: *For everything there is a season, and a time for every matter under heaven.* Our season was up many years ago, but I was trying to hold. Sometimes we have to learn to LET GO and trust God. In Revelations 21:4, it states: *He will wipe away every tear from your eyes, and death shall be no more, neither shall there be mourning, nor crying, nor pain anymore, for the former things have passed away.* My boyfriend and I cried so much that day and I left. I was tired of the hurting, stress, and strain on our child, so I had to let it go.

Steps To Get Out Of An Unhealthy Relationship

1. You first have to decide if you love yourself more than him.

2. Take a break. Find out what makes you happy and if it is meant to be then it will be.

3. After the break if you still feel the same then you need to make the decision on what you want to do. No one can decide this for you.

4. Make arrangement to where you are going after you decide to leave

Dear First Love,

First, let me start off by saying thank you for giving me the greatest gift, our daughter Aniyah. The three years that we spent together were tough, but I would not have wanted to go through any of that with anyone else. When I look back over everything that we went through, I'm thankful that we made it through it. We may not have had that fairy tale ending that we wanted, but we survived.

Let me apologize for not allowing you to be a man. I tore you down every chance that I got and for that I'm sorry. I also want to apologize for putting my hands on you. Neither of us had the right to be abusive. I wish I would have found another way to express my anger other than fighting.

I wish you nothing but the best in life. I have forgiven you for anything that you have done to me as well. I had to release any hurt or hate that I had for you out of my life, so that I will be ready for when God sends my husband to me. Continue to be the best father you can be for your daughter. Take care of you and your family.

Signed,

The mother of your child

Chapter 7: Nothing Left

After my boyfriend and I decided to separate, I packed up all of our things so that Aniyah and I could move back to Georgia. I cried almost the entire ride to Georgia. In my heart of hearts I already knew that things would never be the same again. I was so miserable that I cried every day for the first couple of weeks. I had so many emotions running through my head that I was driving myself crazy. Even though we were unhealthy together I was still dealing with the fact that I still wanted to be with him but as quick as I left was as quick he started talking to someone else. So not only did I have to deal with this move, but now I had to deal with the fact that we were really over this time. I had nothing left but, my daughter.

When I moved I had no money or no job lined up for me. I was applying for jobs everyday but I was not getting any callbacks. What was I going to do? I had a child to take care of. I knew my grandma would help me, but I was grown and got myself in this situation, so I wanted to get out of this alone. I never stop applying for jobs and things were starting to come around for me. One day I went to the mailbox and noticed some mail for me. It was an invitation to come in for training for a substitute teaching position. I was so elated! Anyone that knows me, knows that I don't like being broke. It was killing me to not be able to take care of my child or myself. I never lost the faith because I believed that my better days were on the way.

After the move and the breakup, I thought that my ex and I would be able to co-parent without any drama, but of course it didn't work out like that. We were fussing more and more as the days went on. I already felt that I lost everything I had my house, my boyfriend, and my job. To my surprise I wasn't done losing things out of my life. My daughter's father and family came to Georgia and picked her up. I was crushed. How much more can I take? I begin to ask God why he was doing this to me. My daughter was my world and now she was gone too. I began to have so much hatred in my heart for him and his family because I felt like they were doing this to hurt me more than I already was.

At this point, I was so depressed that I didn't want to talk to anyone or be around anyone. I just wanted to sit at home and mope around. I hated life more than anyone could ever imagine. My family made it their business to let it be known that I needed to get over it. No one knows what I was truly dealing with.

When I didn't have them on my side I always had my ex. When I was up crying at night because I really wanted a better relationship with my family, he was there holding me and wiping my tears away. When I was sick my ex was there nursing me back. He did more for me than most of my family. I will never understand why they felt like it was ok to beat me up when I was already down.

> *"Girl, get over him. He wasn't good for you anyways. You sitting over there crying over someone that doesn't even want you. You lost everything girl you can just start over. You are really getting on my nerves moping around."*

These were the words I continually heard from my family. Guess what? Not one time did someone say, *"Shameka, are you ok?* Is there anything that will make this easier for you? Let me help you get back on your feet. Nothing. At that point, I felt like I was alone and no one understood me. I acted as if everything was ok just for them to leave me alone, but deep down inside I was broken. I wasn't happy and things just weren't getting better.

I was fed up and I got on the phone with my aunt and told her I needed to come back home. At this time, my sister was pregnant with her first child, so I wanted to wait until she gave birth before I left. Unfortunately, my plan was altered when my sister went into early labor and sadly gave birth to a stillborn precious little boy. I was now going back and forth on what I was going to do. Was I going to stay and be there for my sister or was I going back to North Carolina to start my life over and be near my child?

I had to make a selfish decision for myself and my daughter, so I decided to leave. I knew that I couldn't support my sister if I was constantly grieving the separation from my daughter. I never wanted my sister to think that I just didn't care because that was far from the truth. I was torn and wanted to be able to support both of them. Unfortunately, I was in a place in my life where I was damaged and alone. Again, I packed all of my things and those Aniyah's left behind and I told my grandmother that I had to go back to North Carolina. That month that I was in Georgia showed me that no one is going to have my best interest in mind but myself. I learned to never depend on others to validate who I am.

Steps To Get Out Of An Unhealthy Relationship

To get over the hurt that my family took me through I had to:

1. Pray, Let it Go & Know that GOD has you covered.

2. Acknowledge that everyone will not agree with what you are doing.

3. Love from a distance.

4. Stop depending on others to validate who I was.

5. Learn to forgive even when others feel like they haven't done anything wrong.

6. Never show them that you are weak

LIVING WITH SECRETS ~*The Unmasking of the Hidden Identity*

Dear Family Members,

I wanted to let you that when I moved back home, after losing my home for the second time, you did nothing but tear me down. I was on the verge of losing my mind and you didn't even know. I was so broken, but you never gave me the chance to be transparent and share my hurt with you. You beat me up with your words. You cannot possible say that you love me while treating me that way. The last time that I checked, love didn't hurt. For everything that you took me through, God elevated me to the place I'm in right now.

I don't think that you knew I sat in my grandmother's bathroom with a pile of pill bottles rocking back and forward because I was losing my mind and I wanted to die. That same night I had to cry out to God and ask him to cover my mind. I don't think that you knew about the time that I was sitting in my room with a knife to my wrist, getting ready to slice myself and end it all. You were so quick to judge me, but had no idea what I was struggling with behind closed doors. For so long I hated most of you and didn't want to be around you so that's why I secluded myself.

God had to mend my broken heart. Now that I'm no longer broken, I'm able to genuinely forgive each of you. You taught me a lot about this thing called life. Thank you. My past hurt and experiences will allow me to now help others feeling abandoned and isolated.

Family, I am released from you and will continue to love you.

Signed,

The Forgive

Chapter 8: Who Am I?

Once I made it back to North Carolina I didn't reconnect with anyone. I went to work and back home to my daughter. I remember one particular day, I was lounging around the house with my cousin and she told me that one of her friends was coming over and she wanted me to go outside with her. Of course I went outside with her. My cousin and I did everything together. When her friend arrived at my house, a second person got out of the car as well. I gave my cousin the, *I am going to kill you,* look. She introduced me to this young man and my cousin and her friend walked off. I sat down on my porch and he followed. We sat on the porch and talk for hours. For the first time in a long time I was actually smiling.

We exchanged numbers and scheduled our first date. Honestly, he was much older and not my type, but I put all of that to the side because he treated me the way I knew I needed to be treated. That initial date turned into a long-term complicated relationship. Everything was perfect at first. My daughter loved him and so did I. About a year into the relationship, things began to take a turn. I found out that he was living with another woman and the car I was riding around in was hers! She put a tracker on his phone, which led her directly to my house. Even with all this infidelity information, I continued our relationship. We continued until I said we were done. The crazy thing is, every time I said it was over, I would go right back to him.

The final time that I ended it was truly the last. I gave him my whole heart and he stepped all over it, again. Everything started good. He had his own house, so Aniyah and I would spend most of our time there and then he moved into another place. I stayed up late helping him get his house together so he could move in. While we spent a lot of time at his new place, things started changing. He would get missing and stop answering my phone calls. He doesn't know this, but one night I rode pass his house and saw the car of the same woman, from before. While he told me that was over, it wasn't. I wanted to go knock on the door, but my friend held me back. I tried to call him, but he didn't answer.

The next day, he called and asked to take me to lunch and I accepted. We went and he told me everything. He shared that he was living with the women, but it wasn't anything more than just roommates. He promised that he loved me, but couldn't give me what I wanted. Even after all of that, can you believe that I still stayed around? All of this happened near Thanksgiving. We all actually had dinner together. We gathered around a table; me and my daughter and him and his children. I was so dumb for thinking this was ever ok. He was living the life and I was allowing him to do this to me. After this he went back to ignoring me again. I noticed that I was no longer friends with him on social media, but I could still see his page and there it was, the icing on the cake for me, he was dating a whole new woman!

I contacted him and expressed my feelings. He responded by telling me that I will never have enough to bring to this relationship and I don't have nothing and never will. Wow! This was the person I loved. He was absolutely correct. What could I really offer any relationship? I was still living with my aunt. I was working this part-time job barely making enough to do anything with. I couldn't really help that much with bills. My aunt and I were always arguing.

All I kept hearing was all the negative things people had ever said to me. I replayed everything that ever happened to me. All the hurt and all the pain was consuming my life. I had officially lost it. I didn't care about life anymore; I have checked out. I shut down and wouldn't talk to anybody. I would go to work, home, and church. I wouldn't even talk to my pastor. I was drinking, smoking marijuana, and having unprotected sex every day. I was numb and I wanted to die. I felt that no one loved me and I had hurt so many people. Most importantly, I had failed my daughter. My pastor always told me that no matter what you are going through never stop going to church. I kept pressing each Sunday. I was still going through, but I was still showing up at church.

My Steps To Overcoming Depression:

1. Pray

2. Use all the negative things that were said to you as motivation to keep pressing through.

Depression is a serious disease and sometimes it leads to some killing themselves. You will never understand what depression is until you have gone through it. I was living but I was dead on the inside. Sometimes I was smiling but behind the smile I was thinking of jumping off a bridge. I advise you to seek medical help if you can't do it alone. I did it alone but I also had a relationship with God.

Dear Young Man,

I loved you more than life itself and all you did was to continue to hurt me over and over again. You knew more about me than anybody else. You were there for me when no one else was. It wasn't all bad but for the most part it was. I had people tell me how crazy I was for keep falling for you.

Thank you for never treating my daughter any different. You still show her the same caring spirit, to this day. She loves you so much. I am glad that you kept your word and continued to spend time with her. I will never discredit you, as a parent because you are great with your children and mine too.

Thank you for saying all those things that you did to me. I wasn't mad, but I was sad. It's sad because what you said to me was true. It was a wake-up call. I didn't have anything to bring to the relationship but sex and you could get that from anywhere. Your words motivated me to get up and stop being lazy and do something with my life. I wish you nothing but the best. The only thing that I ask is that you never treat another woman like you did me because the next outcome might be very different.

Signed,
The Believer

Chapter 9:
Mending My Broken Heart

My former pastor saved my life. When I started going to the church I was broken. No one knew me but my former pastor and I didn't know anyone. My former pastor sat down with me and I was able to be myself. I just laid myself out to her explaining to her how bad I needed her and God. She never judged me and I was very open with her. I knew then that she was someone that I could trust with my life. My former pastor never stopped praying for me. I prayed and asked God to send me someone to help me because I couldn't do it alone. He sent my former pastor. I call her my life-saver because when I was unable to seek God for myself, she was on her knees interceding for me. The whole time that I was still dealing with my depression I was still going to church.

One particular church service changed my life for forever. I will never forget my former pastor talking about how we hold ourselves back because we are always making excuses and waiting for somebody to hand it to us. The whole time that I was there I showed no interest in the service, but when I got home God worked on me. I went in my room as soon as I got home from church and I got down on my knees and ask God if he gets me out of this depression, I would never go back. I also asked God to show me what I should be doing with my life and he showed me. From that day forward I have not experience depression again.

God showed me Daughters of Divine Destiny. He gave it to me when I was 18, but I never did anything with it because I felt like I was too young and I wasn't equipped enough to do it. God told me to step out on faith and do it. I did just that. I was determined to fight through the pain, the hurt, and the disappointment to reach my destiny, while blessing and inspiring other girls fighting through the same things that I did. I was up early and I stayed up all night because I wasn't going to rest until I made my dream a reality. I started to write out my vision for this nonprofit, the mission and who I wanted to inspire. I had a lot of roadblocks and the devil wanted me to give up, but I still kept going. My finances were all jacked up but I said if I keep using that as an excuse then I will never do it, so I pressed forward. It was time for me to stop being scared and do what I was called to do and have wanted to do for over ten years. One thing that I now know for sure is that if there is something that you really want to do, you must step out on faith and do it! God will always take care of the rest.

I vowed to myself that once I released everything that I was not going back. Ever since I was a little girl all I knew was hurt and pain. I had to release the secrets that held me bound; even those that I knew would hurt some. I had to accept that everyone was not going to support my change, but I could no longer worry about others being hurt or upset. I was working towards my own freedom and not looking back. I was ready to start my life over again and I was excited. God gave the desire of my heart and freed me from my personal bondage. When you are truly free, you feel lighter. You feel like the bondage that you have been carrying, for so many years, has finally been lifted. No more sleepless nights., I AM FREE! No more thoughts of suicide, I AM FREE! No more days of hating myself, I AM FREE!

I remember the day that I was freed just like it was yesterday. The night before I sent out emails and phone calls to those individuals that I was holding secrets from. Some of my secrets went back over eighteen years. I released all of it. I stripped the hurt and shame and released my truth to everyone. Some responded and some didn't. I cried most of the night out of shock and relief that I had finally shared. I felt bad because I hurt someone that was really close to me. I never wanted to hurt anyone but I had to be free. I needed these weights lifted off of me. The shackles had to be freed.

The next morning, I felt so much better. I was happier than I have been in a very long time. The feeling that I felt was as if I was walking on air. I told myself that God released me and I will not and cannot ever let anyone dictate my life like I have done in the past. Once you become free, stay free! It is one of the greatest feelings in the world. You will no longer have the strongholds of others that stop you from reaching your full potential. I'm free and today I pray that you will be free as well. Once I let go and let God, I learned how to live again. I had to learn how to love myself before I was able to love anyone else. I found myself alone a lot because I had to get to know me all over again. I know this may sound crazy to some, but it's a process. I lost who I was in the mist of everything that was going on. I let people run over me and pour so much negativity into my life that I believed it. I had to be restored.

In my process I lost a lot of friends because they didn't understand what I was going through. I secluded myself and they didn't understand the transformation that I was undergoing. From their perspective, they were inviting me places and I kept turning them down. During this process I stop dating and I started taking myself out on dates because I wanted to get past the fear of going out alone. Each morning, when I would wake up, I would say a prayer, look in the mirror and recite my affirmation. I had to say them until I believed them for myself.

My values and views changed. I started to put Shameka before others. Outside of my daughter, I became my biggest priority. I made a promise to myself that I will no longer be stressed or depressed. I don't hold on to what people say to or about me. I walk in my own confidence. I know who I am now and I'm unstoppable. What makes me unstoppable? Well, let me tell you, I'm unstoppable because even though I went through things in my life that could have taken my life, I didn't let that stop me. I actually used those things to motivate me to do better. I'm a go-getter.

Once I realized who I was and what I was worth things begin to change in my life. I have so much life to live and it begin when I was released. My daughter deserves better and that's what I'm going to give her. I had to go through everything to end up at this moment, to end up at my happy place.

Final Freedom Revelations:

Here are some nuggets for you, as you seek your own freedom and release:

- Let go of the fear
- Find a way to release yourself from people that may have hurt you (letter, email, phone call, etc.)
- Understand that it's not your fault
- Seek professional help
- Pray, Cry, and Pray some more
- Forgive
- Move on
- Find who you are
- Live life to the fullest you owe it to yours

Today, I am the founder of my own youth group called *Daughters of Divine Destiny*, where we focus on empowering and encouraging young girls. I trained to become a Certified Life Coach and am now the CEO of *Serenity Love Coaching* as well as *Impact Youth Newsletter*. I also host a radio segment on Mocha Live Inspirational radio called *Affirmations and Inspirations*.

If I had to leave something with you it would be this: **Never let fear stop you from telling your story.** It wasn't until I let go of fear that I was able to share my story and move on with my life. I have **RELEASED MY SECRETS** and I want the same thing for you as well.

FOLLOW SHAMEKA AT: FACEBOOK- @SHAMEKALECOUNT

FOR COPIES & BOOKING INFORMATION, EMAIL: SLECOUNT@LIVE.COM

www.ingramcontent.com/pod-product-compliance
Lightning Source LLC
Chambersburg PA
CBHW071737090426
42738CB00011B/2509